A Little

Coffee

Cookbook

Janet Laurence

ILLUSTRATED BY CATHERINE McWILLIAMS

Appletree Press

First published in 1992 by
The Appletree Press Ltd,
7 James Street South, Belfast BT2 8DL.
Copyright © 1992 The Appletree Press, Ltd.
Illustrations © 1992 The Appletree Press, Ltd.
Printed in the E.C. All rights reserved.
No part of this publication may be reproduced
or transmitted in any form or by means,
electronic or mechanical, photocopying,
recording or any information and retrieval
system, without permission in writing from
the publisher.

A Little Coffee Cookbook

A catalogue record for this book is available
in The British Library.

ISBN: 0-86281-328-X

9 8 7 6 5 4 3

A note on measures
Metric, imperial and volume measurements
have been given for all the recipes. Use one
set only. Spoon measurements are level.
Recipes are for four, unless
otherwise indicated.

Introduction

Coffee offers a rich and potent experience. Its powerful and haunting flavour and aroma are instantly recognisable yet, so many and so varied are the blends offered, few cups are the same. Its mystique confounds many but making a good cup of coffee is simplicity itself. Its powers of stimulation can be as addictive as its lively and subtle flavour; coffee is the thinking person's drink and one of the sophisticated cook's favourite flavourings. Coffee first grew wild in Ethiopia. Originally a kind of wine made from the fermented bean pulp, it was known by the poetic Arabic word for wine, "qahweh". Later the beans were roasted and pulverised and the powder whipped into hot water. Coffee offered stimulation without the taint of forbidden alcohol and pilgrims spread its use throughout the Islamic world.

The Venetians brought coffee to Europe in 1615, with instant success. Over the next hundred years, coffee houses opened in many major cities, providing meeting places for businessmen, politicians, journalists, artists and intellectuals. Revolutions were said to have been fermented in cafes, commercial institutions grew out of them and they became fashionable centres for refreshment and gossip. In America, the Tea Tax and the Boston Tea Party linked coffee indelibly in the American mind with liberty and democracy.

Coffee has been claimed to be both beneficial and harmful. Caffeine in small doses can improve attention, concentration and co-ordination and, in excess, can produce over-acute sensations, irregular heartbeats and muscular trembling. Like most great things in life, coffee is best enjoyed in moderation.

The Cultivation of Coffee

The Arabs tried to maintain a monopoly on the production of coffee by refusing to allow plants or unsterilized berries to leave their shores but seeds and small plants were soon smuggled out. In the seventeenth century, coffee began to be grown in India and the Far East Dutch colonies such as Java and Ceylon. Later it reached the West Indies and South America where Brazil in particular provided ideal conditions.

In the second half of the nineteenth century, *Hemileia vastatrix,* a devastating leaf disease, struck Asia and moved on to Africa, wiping out the coffee trees. Brazil took over as pre-eminent grower, a position it maintained after cultivation was re-established in Africa and Asia and still holds today, when coffee is grown wherever there is a suitable climate.

There are two species of coffee tree. *Coffee arabica* is the original and produces beans of a more complex, interesting flavour. *Coffee canephora,* also known as *robusta,* is easier to cultivate and can be grown in warmer and lower regions; it is used mainly in some instant coffees. Roughly speaking, the higher coffee is grown, the better its flavour.

Coffee trees resemble laurel bushes and bear beautiful, sweet smelling white flowers at the same time as the berries are ripening. Each berry usually contains two flat-sided seeds or beans. A single bean is round, known as a peaberry. Picked when red and about the size of a cherry, the berry pulp has to be softened so the beans can be separated before being cleaned, dried, graded and then shipped.

Coffee's distinctive flavour and colour are developed by roasting, a process which needs nice judgement and varies according to the desired taste. Different coffee varieties

yield different degrees of aroma, body, acidity and colour and expert tasters develop blends to suit different tastes and purposes.

Roasting Degrees
Light or pale: mild coffee with a delicate flavour, good with milk and ideal for breakfast.
Medium: more character with a stronger flavour.
Full or dark: a strong, full-bodied flavour.
High, double or continental: very strong, accentuates coffee's bitter aspects and often loses some of the original flavour, should be drunk black.

Varieties
Today over fifty countries produce more than 100 varieties of coffee. Specialist shops offer carefully selected blends of arabica beans, some of the best come from:
Brazil: Most prized is Santos, a sweet, clear, neutral flavour.
Columbia: The Andes foothills produces some of the finest coffees. Look for: Medellins, Excelso, Manizales, Armenias, Libanos, Bogotas and Bucaramangas.
Costa Rica: Excellent coffees, particularly those from the Central Plateau, with a rich body and fine, mild flavour.
Jamaica: High grown Blue Mountain is most expensive and highly prized coffee in the world.
Kenya: Excellent flavour and fine acidity, the Peaberry's round shape allows for even roasting.
Mocha: The Yemeni seaport from which coffee was first exported gave its name to highly popular Ethiopian beans.
Mysore: Indian coffees with a distinctive, soft, acid flavour.
Decaffeinated: Recently popular, available varieties have increased and flavour has improved. The caffeine is removed either through steaming (the Swiss method) or a solvent.

Instant: Freshly brewed liquid is either evaporated or freeze dried, the latter is considered to give the better result.
Organic: A tiny proportion of the coffee available but a rapidly growing market.

Making Coffee

Coffee's flavour comes from volatile oils that start deteriorating immediately after roasting and grinding accelerates the process. So buy in small quantities and, if possible, grind just before using or keep opened packets tightly closed. Vacuum packs conserve flavour, so does keeping in the freezer. Maximum flavour comes from steeping coffee grounds for two minutes in water at a temperature just below boiling. As a general rule, use one tablespoon of grounds per 100 ml/3 fl oz/scant 1/2 cup of freshly drawn water. Dilute with hot water or milk for weaker coffee. Drink as soon as possible, flavour and aroma are both volatile. Keep equipment spotlessly clean, coffee oil residue turns rancid.

Jug or cafetière: Simplest of all methods. Warm either, add medium ground coffee, pour on hot water. When using a jug give a good stir, leave two minutes then strain or spoon over a little cold water to settle grounds. With a cafetière, leave two minutes then slowly push down plunger, never force it.
Filter: Fit special filter paper into the cone, place on top of a jug, add finely ground coffee and a little hot water to moisten. Then slowly pour on rest of hot water. Electric machines are available but some over-extract coffee and give a bitter flavour. Single portion "cafe filters" should be placed over a warmed cup.

Drip: A three-part coffee jug. Place finely ground coffee in middle, pour hot water in the top and allow to filter through to the bottom part. A metal kind allows the water to be heated on the stove, then the pot is reversed for the filter process.

Cona: Two glass bowls are connected via a glass funnel and filter and held in a stand over a spirit lamp. The water is heated in the bottom bowl to boiling point, when it rises into the upper bowl, which holds finely ground coffee. Give it a good stir, remove the heat and allow the coffee to filter through to the bottom bowl. Remove top bowl before serving.

Percolator: Place medium ground coffee in the basket, fill percolator with fresh water and heat until steam forces the water repeatedly through the stem and over the coffee. Electric percolators time the process automatically. Purists maintain this method over-extracts the coffee, producing a bitter result.

Espresso: A mixture of steam and water at higher temperature then normal is forced through very finely ground coffee, producing a stronger brew than the above methods and a layer of froth. Cappuccino adds a mixture of hot milk and steam; grated chocolate or cinnamon is almost always added as a finishing touch.

Turkish and Arabian: A strong, slightly bitter coffee that is usually served sweetened. Boil 2 teaspoons of sugar (or to taste) with one small coffee cup of water in either a traditional *ibrik*, a small brass pot with a narrow top and long handle, or a small saucepan. Add 2 teaspoons very finely ground coffee, stirring well. Heat again until the coffee froths up, remove pot from heat and allow to settle then repeat twice more. Allow to settle again then serve. A cardamom pod or a clove or two or a pinch of freshly grated nutmeg can be added to the water before boiling.

Coffee Drinks

Iced Coffee. There are more ways of drinking coffee than straight and hot. Iced coffee can be made by cooling a freshly made brew in the refrigerator then serving to taste with sugar, or honey, and cream. But on really hot days it is most refreshing made extra strong and poured over ice cubes.

---

freshly made, double strength coffee
equal quantity ice cubes
sugar or honey to taste
cream

Make the coffee, allow to cool, then pour over ice cubes, sweeten to taste with sugar or honey then add cream and stir.

Spiced Coffee. Most spirits and liqueurs accompany coffee beautifully and a number will lace it equally well. Add sugar, even if you normally take coffee without, the spirit makes it bitter otherwise. This is the ultimate alcoholic coffee.

---

125 ml/4 fl oz/^{1}/$_2$ cup brandy
3 tbsp sugar
10 whole cloves, 5 cm/^{1}/$_2$ in piece cinnamon stick
thinly pared peel of I lemon and I orange
one third of a vanilla bean
I litre/I ^{1}/$_2$ pints/4 cups black coffee, freshly made
(serves 6–8 people)

Place all the ingredients except the coffee, which should be kept hot, in a stainless steel or enamel saucepan and heat gently until sugar dissolved and brandy warm enough to light. Ignite then pour coffee over, warm through if necessary, and strain into coffee cups.

Irish Coffee. If Spiced Coffee is the ultimate, Irish is the favourite after-dinner alcoholic coffee, simple but utterly delicious. I remember a bar in San Francisco in the sixties that lined up the glassed along the counter to make twenty or so Irish Coffees at a time. Don't use too delicate a glass and choose a medium-dark roast for your coffee, otherwise the flavour of the whisky will prove too powerful.

I hefty wine goblet, warmed
2 tbsp Irish whisky
I tsp, or more, of brown sugar
freshly-brewed strong, medium-dark roast coffee
2 tbsp double cream
(makes I)

Place the whisky in the bottom of the glass, add the sugar and place a spoon in the glass. Pour the coffee over the spoon and stir to dissolve the sugar. Hold the spoon just above the level of the coffee, rounded side up, and carefully pour over the cream so it floats on the surface of the coffee. Don't stir, the idea is to drink the whisky-fortified coffee through the smooth richness of the cream. Heaven.

Caffe Sambuca. The Italians have a special trick with their liqueur Sambuca, made from liquorice and elderflower.

I liqueur glass Sambuca
3 or 5 dark roasted coffee beans
(makes I)

Float the coffee beans on top of the liqueur. Light with a match and allow to burn for a few seconds then blow out (be gentle) and sip the liqueur which is now faintly flavoured with freshly-roasted coffee. The *cognoscenti* crunch the beans as they sip.

Marinated Mushrooms

Full of a robust and tantalising flavour, these mushrooms make a good starter or side salad.

8oz/225g button mushrooms, trimmed
3 tbsp fresh lemon juice
8 fl oz/250ml/1 cup medium-strength black coffee
3 tbsp groundnut, peanut or arachide oil
small bunch parsley stalks, a sprig thyme
and 1 celery stalk, all tied together
1 tsp coriander seeds
2 crushed cloves garlic
1/2 tsp salt, little freshly-ground black pepper
freshly chopped parsley

Add mushrooms and lemon juice to a saucepan of boiling water and blanch for five minutes. Drain and refresh in cold water. Bring remaining ingredients, apart from the chopped parsley, to boil and simmer gently for five minutes. Add the drained mushrooms, bring back to boil then remove from heat, place in suitable container and leave to marinate at least six hours or, better, overnight. Sprinkle with chopped parsley before serving with crusty bread or wholemeal toast.

Coffee and Chestnut Pâté

A pâté with an interesting texture and a subtle, autumnal flavour.

---

1 small onion, finely chopped
1 clove garlic, crushed
1 tbsp groundnut, peanut or arachide oil
2 celery stalks, finely chopped
12oz/350g cooked chestnuts, roughly chopped
15oz/425g tin unsweetened chestnut purée
7 tbsp strong black coffee
2 eggs, lightly beaten
little salt, freshly-ground black pepper
bay leaf
(serves 8)

Gently fry the onion and garlic in the oil until soft. Mix with the celery and chopped chestnuts.

Mix together the chestnut purée, coffee, eggs and seasoning. Stir in the chopped chestnut mixture.

Grease a 2 lb/1 kg loaf tin or round dish of similar volume and place the bay leaf in the bottom. Add the pâté mixture, pressing down firmly. Cover with two layers of foil, fastening it round the edges of the dish. Place pâté in a roasting tin and add sufficient cold water to come halfway up the loaf tin. Bake in a pre-heated oven at gas mark 3, 325°F, 160°C for 1 1/2–2 hours. Remove mould from heat and leave to cool on a rack for several hours before turning out.

Spicy Chicken

The coffee combines with the spices and liver to make a rich, fragrant sauce that defies analysis. Freshly-ground spices will improve the flavour.

---

1 chicken, 3 1/2 lbs/1 1/2 kg, jointed, reserve liver
1 tsp powdered cinnamon
1 tsp ground cumin
pinch ground mace
10 fl oz/300ml black coffee, medium strong
salt
2 tbsp cream, preferably double
2oz/50g toasted almonds

Mix together the spices and rub over the surface of the chicken pieces. Place in a plastic bag, pour over the strained coffee and arrange the bag in a bowl so that the chicken is immersed in the coffee. Leave in a cool place overnight.

Place chicken leg pieces in a shallow roasting dish, pour over the marinade, add salt and cook, uncovered, in a pre-heated oven at gas mark 4, 350°F, 180°C for 15 minutes, then baste and add breast pieces and the liver and continue cooking for another 30 minutes, or until chicken is cooked, basting with the coffee juices.

Remove the cooked chicken and keep warm. Skim juices of all fat then process or sieve with the cooked liver. Pour into a clean pan, adjust seasoning then reheat to just below boiling point. Stir in the cream, remove from heat and pour over the chicken. Garnish with the toasted almonds and serve.

Lamb Roasted With Coffee

This is a traditional Swedish recipe. The coffee cuts the fatty quality of the lamb and produces delicious gravy but is quite unrecognisable in the finished dish.

---

4 1/2 lb/2 kg leg of lamb
little butter or oil
salt and freshly-ground black pepper
10 fl oz/300ml/generous cup coffee, medium strength, mixed
with 2 tbsp single cream and 1 tsp sugar
Sauce:
2 tbsp flour
additional single cream or milk
1 tsp redcurrant jelly
(serves 6)

Rub meat with butter or oil, season well. Place in roasting tin and roast in pre-heated oven at gas mark 6, 400°F, 200°C for 10 minutes. Reduce heat to gas mark 4, 350°F, 180°C and continue roasting for one hour, basting every 20 minutes. Then add the white, sweetened coffee to the pan and continue roasting for another hour, or until joint cooked to your liking, basting as before. When done, remove meat and keep warm.

Strain the pan juices then skim fat off the top and return 2 tablespoons to the roasting pan with the 2 tablespoons of flour. Cook over a moderate heat on the hob for a few minutes, stirring all the time, then make a smooth sauce with the degreased juices and redcurrant jelly, made up to 15 fl oz/375 ml/2 cups with additional single cream or milk, scraping the bottom of the roasting pan well to incorporate any crusty bits with all their flavour. Adjust seasoning, simmer 5–10 minutes then serve with the meat.

Coffee Cheesecake

This is a cooked cheesecake, rich and really scrumptious, with the coffee and cheese blending perfectly.

Base:

8oz/225g/2 cups digestive/ wheatmeal biscuits, crushed
4oz/100g/1 stick butter, melted
pinch ground cinnamon

5 fl oz/150ml/²/₃ cup double cream
¹/₂ tsp vanilla essence
1¹/₂ tbsp coffee essence

Filling:

1¹/₄ lb/500g/2 ¹/₂ cups curd or cream cheese
8oz/225g/1 cup caster sugar
3 eggs, well beaten

Topping:

5 fl oz/150ml/generous ¹/₂ cup (1 carton) soured cream
1 tbsp caster sugar

(serves 8)

Mix together the crushed biscuits, melted butter and ground cinnamon and use to line the bottom of a greased 8 in / 20 cm diameter tin with a removable base and, if possible, a spring-clip side.

Cream together cheese and sugar, then gradually beat in the eggs. Stir in the cream, the vanilla and the coffee essence. Pour onto the base and bake in a pre-heated oven at gas mark 3, 325°F, 170°C for 30 minutes, until the filling is set. Turn off the oven and leave to cool.

To finish, mix together the soured cream and sugar and spread over the top of the cheesecake. Heat oven to gas mark 7, 425°F, 220°C then bake the cheesecake for about 5 minutes, until the topping has formed a glaze. Remove and chill for several hours, preferably overnight. Carefully release from tin before serving.

Petits Pôts de Crème au Mocha

The Venetians invented the exquisite combination of coffee and chocolate, calling it *mocha*. A full-bodied but mild coffee is best for this recipe.

---

15 fl oz/450ml/2 cups full-cream milk
2 tbsp coffee, coarsely ground
2oz/50g bitter chocolate, broken into pieces
3 tbsp caster sugar
5 large egg yolks

Heat the milk and coffee to just below boiling point, remove from heat, cover and allow to infuse for several minutes. Strain through a fine sieve. Add the sugar and the pieces of chocolate and stir until the chocolate is thoroughly melted. Add the milk mixture to the egg yolks, stirring in at the same time. Pour the egg mixture into ramekin dishes or little custard pots, covering with lids if available (the pots will probably hold more custard than the ramekins). Place in a roasting pan and add cold water to just above half way up the pots. Place in a pre-heated oven at gas mark 3, 325°F, 160°C for 40—50 minutes until the custards are set. A little cream poured over the top before serving is delicious.

Coffee and Ginger Soufflé

The combination of coffee and ginger is excellent, providing a sophisticated dessert.

---

scant half pint/250ml/1 cup full-cream milk
3 tbsp coarsely ground medium-strength coffee
1¹/₂oz/40g/3 tbsp butter
1¹/₂oz/40g/4 tbsp flour
4 egg yolks
6 tbsp caster sugar
3 tbsp chopped stem or crystallised ginger
5 egg whites and a pinch of salt
little icing sugar

Heat the milk with the coffee to boiling point, remove from the heat, cover and allow to infuse for several minutes, then strain. Melt the butter, stir in the flour and cook gently for a few minutes then gradually add the hot coffee-flavoured milk, stirring constantly. Beat the egg yolks until pale then beat into the coffee base. Stir in sugar, then fold in chopped ginger. Whip egg whites with the pinch of salt to stiff peak, fold one third into base to lighten, give whites another quick whisk, add to the base and fold in carefully. Turn soufflé into a 2³/₄ pint/1500ml/scant 7 cups straight-sided ovenproof dish that has been well-buttered and sprinkled with sugar.

Bake in pre-heated oven at gas mark 6, 400°F, 200°C for about 30 minutes. The soufflé is done if it trembles rather than wobbles when gently shaken. Dust with icing sugar and serve immediately accompanied with single cream.

Coffee and Rum Jelly

Sparkling and light and very simple.

---

3 tbsp rum or coffee flavour liqueur
1 tbsp powdered gelatine
1 pt/600ml/2 1/2 cups fresh, well-flavoured coffee
sugar to taste
whipped cream to serve

Place the rum or liqueur in a cup or small dish, sprinkle the gelatine powder over and leave until granules have absorbed the liquid, some five minutes. Have the coffee freshly made and strained if necessary. Add the now transparent gelatine and stir into the coffee with sugar to taste until both are completely dissolved. Pour into clear glasses and chill until set. Serve with lightly-whipped cream, either on the side or poured on top. Variations: The rum or liqueur can be omitted and the gelatine soaked in water. Also, the coffee can be infused with spices; use a piece of cinnamon bark, 2 cloves and 3 allspice berries, omit rum.

Coffee and Rum Mousse

A deliciously light mousse that marries the coffee and rum flavours marvellously.

---

4 tbsp light rum
1/2 oz/15g/1 tbsp powdered gelatine
8 fl oz/250ml/1 cup freshly-made strong
medium roast coffee
3 egg yolks
3oz/75g/6 tbsp caster sugar
8 fl oz/250ml/1 cup double cream
3 egg whites
(serves 6)

Sprinkle gelatine over rum and leave until the powder has absorbed the liquid, about five minutes. Strain the hot coffee, add the soaked gelatine and stir until completely dissolved. Beat the yolks until thick and pale, beat in the sugar until the mixture has increased in volume and is even paler. Gradually beat in the hot liquid and leave to cool. When the mixture has started to thicken, whip the cream until it almost holds its shape then fold in carefully. Whip the egg whites to soft peak and fold in as well. Pour mixture into a 2 pint/1 1/4 litre/ 5 cup mould, or individual dishes, and leave in a cold place to set. Alternatively, use a smaller, 1 1/4 pint/750ml/3 cup mould with a paper collar tied firmly around its top. After the mousse has set, the collar can be removed, leaving the mixture standing proud of the dish, like a risen soufflé. Grated chocolate and/or whipped cream can be used to decorate the mousse. Instead of rum, cognac or kirsch can be used for flavouring.

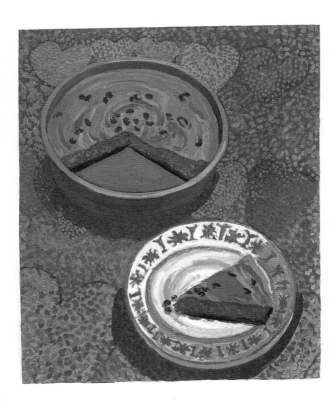

Coffee Chiffon Tart

The crisp shell of this tart contrasts deliciously with a smooth and light filling, the coffee liqueur adding extra flavour.

Crust:	
6oz/175g/1⅓ cup plain chocolate digestive biscuits, crushed	3 egg yolks
	4oz/100g/½ cup caster sugar
3oz/50g/6 tbsp butter, melted	3 tbsp coffee essence
Filling:	3 tbsp Tia Maria
½oz/15g/1 tbsp powdered gelatine	3 egg whites
	Garnish:
4 tbsp water	grated chocolate

(serves 6–8)

Stir together the crushed digestive biscuits and melted butter, then use to coat bottom and sides of a 9 x 1 in / 23 x 2.5 cm deep tart tin or pie dish. Leave to set.

Sprinkle the gelatine over the water in a small saucepan and allow the powder to absorb the water, then heat very gently until the soaked gelatine has melted. Do not allow to boil.

Beat the egg yolks until thick and pale then gradually beat in the sugar until the mixture has swelled in volume and is even paler. Beat in coffee essence and Tia Maria spoon by spoon then add the melted gelatine. As soon as mixture is on the point of setting, whip egg whites to a soft peak and fold in carefully. Fill the chocolate shell and leave in a cool place to set for at least 2 hours. Decorate with grated chocolate and serve with single cream if liked.

Bananas Tia Maria

A very easy dessert loved by everyone who likes bananas.

---

6 firm bananas	*4 tbsp freshly made*
2 tbsp unsalted butter	*strong black coffee*
4 tbsp soft brown sugar	*single cream to serve*
4 tbsp Tia Maria	

Peel the bananas, cut in half lengthwise, place in an ovenproof dish. Melt the butter and pour over the bananas, rolling the fruit so each is covered in butter. Sprinkle the sugar over and place in a pre-heated oven at gas mark 3, 325°F, 160°C for 20 minutes, or until bananas are soft, then remove. Pour off all the juices into a small pan, keep the bananas hot, add the Tia Maria to the pan, set alight and douse with the coffee. Serve immediately with single cream.

Chocolate Marquise
with Coffee Bean Sauce

This is a very rich but utterly delicious dessert that is transformed by the Coffee Bean Sauce.

3oz/75g plain chocolate	*36 sponge fingers*
4 large egg yolks	*5 tbsp strong black coffee*
5oz/125g/^{1}/$_2$ cup caster sugar	**Sauce:**
6oz/175g/^{3}/$_4$ cup unsalted	*12 ^{1}/$_2$ fl oz/375ml/1 ^{1}/$_2$*
butter, softened	*cups full-cream milk*

3oz/75g/⅔ cup unsweetened
cocoa powder, sifted
10 fl oz/300ml/1¼ cups
whipping cream
2 tbsp icing sugar, sifted

5oz/125g/generous ½
cup caster sugar
1½ tsp fresh, fine coffee
grounds
5 medium size egg yolks

(serves 6–8)

Melt chocolate carefully in small bowl over simmering water then remove from heat. Beat egg yolks until pale and fluffy, add sugar gradually, continuing to beat until mixture very pale and thick. Beat in the melted chocolate. Cream butter until light and fluffy then gradually beat in the cocoa powder. Beat together with the chocolate mixture. In a large, chilled bowl, use a balloon whisk to whip together the cream and the icing sugar until very light and thick, be careful not to overbeat. With the whisk, work cream mixture into the chocolate mixture until perfectly blended.

Line a 2 lb/1 kg bread tin with siliconised paper. Brush each sponge finger with the coffee and use to line sides and bottom of tin or mould. Fill centre with the chocolate mixture and chill in refrigerator for 2–3 hours.

For the sauce, place milk and half the sugar in a saucepan and bring to boiling point. Add the coffee grounds, cover, remove from heat and leave to infuse for 15 minutes. Beat egg yolks until pale and thick, add remaining sugar and beat again until increased in volume and even paler. Continue to beat while adding the milk and coffee mixture. Clean out saucepan, add custard mixture and cook over a very low heat, stirring constantly, until it thickens. To test: dip wooden spatula or spoon into mixture, hold up and run a finger across the custard. If channel remains clear, the custard is cooked. Do not let the custard boil or it will curdle. Cool, stirring.

Turn Marquise out onto serving plate and accompany with sauce.

Café Parfait

The best, the creamiest, the tastiest of ices.

---

8 fl oz/250ml/I cup single cream
4 tbsp medium ground coffee
4 egg yolks
4oz/100g/¹/₂ cup caster sugar
8 fl oz/250ml/I cup double cream

Heat single cream to boiling point, add the ground coffee, stir well, cover, remove from heat and leave to infuse for 15 minutes.

Beat the egg yolks until thick and pale, gradually beat in the sugar and continue beating until mixture forms a thick "ribbon" when the beater is held up. Continue to beat while adding the cream and coffee, then pour into a clean saucepan and cook gently over a very low heat, stirring all the time, until mixture is slightly thickened. To test: Dip wooden spoon or spatula into mixture, hold up and run a finger through the custard coating. If the channel remains clear, the custard is cooked. Strain custard into a bowl and leave to cool.

Beat double cream until it will nearly hold its shape then fold carefully into cooled custard mixture. Either freeze in ice cream maker or freeze in a metal tray, beating the mixture well once or twice as it freezes.

Granita al Caffe

The most refreshing of desserts, very popular in Italy. Make sure the coffee has a lively flavour.

A Little Coffee Cookbook

Janet Laurence

ILLUSTRATED BY CATHERINE McWILLIAMS

Gâteau Malakoff au Café

Richest of all coffee puddings and quite irresistible.

praline made with 6oz/150g/
1¼ cups browned hazelnuts
and 6oz/175g/²/₃ cup
caster sugar
6oz/175g/2 sticks unsalted
butter, softened
6oz/175g/1¹/₃ cups icing
sugar, sifted
1 large egg yolk

3 tbsp best instant coffee
dissolved in 5 tbsp
water just off the boil
15 fl oz/450ml/2 cups
whipping cream
27 sponge fingers
3 tbsp Tia Maria or
Kahlua
5 fl oz/150ml/²/₃ cup milk
toasted almond halves

(serves 8–10)

Make praline by heating sugar over brisk heat until it first
melts then turns brown. Add the nuts, stir well then turn out
onto an oiled tin or piece of marble. Allow to cool completely
then break into small bits and grind either in a processor or
small mill.

Cream butter then beat in sugar bit by bit until mixture is
very light and fluffy. Beat in the egg yolk and then the coffee.
Stir in the praline mixture. Whip the cream until it just holds
its shape and fold carefully into the coffee butter icing.

Mix together the liqueur and the milk, then briefly dip both
sides of nine sponge fingers and arrange them in threes on the
base of an oblong serving dish; spread over a layer of the
cream. Repeat with two more layers of biscuits and cream.
Finally use the remaining cream to cover the sides of the block.
Scatter the toasted almonds over the top, then chill for
several hours, preferably overnight, before serving.

Appletree Press

generous 1 1/2 pt/1 ltr/4 cups freshly brewed strong coffee
8 tbsp caster sugar
3 tbsp rum
8 fl oz/250ml/1 cup whipping cream
2 tbsp icing sugar, sifted
(serves 6)

Add the sugar to the hot coffee and stir until dissolved. Allow to cool then stir in the rum. Pour into large metal container, or containers, so that there is only a shallow depth of liquid, this will help speed the freezing. Place in freezer. When solid, plunge bottom of container into boiling water for a few seconds then turn out frozen coffee and break into pieces. Process into small crystals. Return to freezer until ready to serve. Whip cream with the icing sugar until it holds its shape. Remove crystals from freezer and, if necessary, briefly process again, then pile into six chilled serving glasses, top with whipped cream and serve immediately.

Walnut and Coffee Roulade

An impressive dessert that is always popular.

Roulade:	Filling:
5 large eggs, separated	3 egg yolks
5oz/125g/generous 1/2 cup caster sugar	4oz/100g/scant 1/2 cup caster sugar
3oz/75g/scant cup walnuts, ground quite finely	3 tbsp cornflour
2 tbsp cornflour	8 fl oz/250ml/1 cup boiling milk
	1 small knob of butter
	2 tbsp coffee essence

(serves 6)

Line a Swiss roll tin approximately 13 x 8 in / 32 x 20 cm with siliconised, non-stick paper. Beat egg yolks until pale then beat in sugar until thick and almost white. Mix ground walnuts with cornflour and fold into beaten yolks. Whip egg white to stiff peak stage and fold into walnut mixture lightly but thoroughly. Pour into prepared tin and bake 20 minutes in oven pre-heated to gas mark 4, 350°F, 180°C until well risen, golden and resilient to touch. Turn out onto sheet of greaseproof paper sprinkled with sugar and remove lining paper (tear it off in strips if it starts to stick). Trim long edges with very sharp knife, roll roulade and paper up loosely together from one of the short ends and leave on rack to cool.

To make *crème pâtissière* filling, beat egg yolks then beat in sugar until the mixture is thick and pale. Beat in the cornflour. Gradually pour on the boiling milk while continuing to beat. Pour mixture into clean saucepan and place over a medium heat. Bring to the boil while stirring continuously with a wire whisk but be careful mixture doesn't burn on bottom of the pan. After mixture has reached boiling point, lower heat and simmer very gently for 2—3 minutes, watching that it doesn't scorch. Then remove from heat and beat in a knob of butter with the coffee essence. Cover with cling film and leave to cool.

When the filling is cold, carefully unroll the roulade, spread the *crème pâtissière* over and roll up again, making a firm pleat with the beginning then using the paper to pull the roll over, finally landing it on a serving dish (don't worry if the roll splits, it looks good with some of the filling oozing out). Sift a little icing sugar over before serving.

Gâteau Malakoff au Café

Richest of all coffee puddings and quite irresistible.

---

*praline made with 6oz/150g/
1 1/4 cups browned hazelnuts
and 6oz/175g/3/4 cup
caster sugar
6oz/175g/2 sticks unsalted
butter, softened
6oz/175g/1/3 cups icing
sugar, sifted
1 large egg yolk*

*3 tbsp best instant coffee
dissolved in 5 tbsp
water just off the boil
15 fl oz/450ml/2 cups
whipping cream
27 sponge fingers
3 tbsp Tia Maria or
Kahlua
5 fl oz/150ml/2/3 cup milk
toasted almond halves*

(serves 8–10)

Make praline by heating sugar over brisk heat until it first melts then turns brown. Add the nuts, stir well then turn out onto an oiled tin or piece of marble. Allow to cool completely then break into small bits and grind either in a food processor or small mill.

Cream butter then beat in sugar bit by bit until mixture is very light and fluffy. Beat in the egg yolk and then the coffee. Stir in the praline mixture. Whip the cream until it just holds its shape and fold carefully into the coffee butter icing.

Mix together the liqueur and the milk then briefly dip both sides of nine sponge fingers and arrange them in threes on the base of an oblong serving dish; spread over a layer of the cream. Repeat with two more layers of biscuits and cream. Finally use the remaining cream to cover the sides of the block. Scatter the toasted almonds over the top then chill for several hours, preferably overnight, before serving.

Coffee Meringue Gâteau

A crisp and delectable gâteau to serve with coffee or tea or as a dessert.

Meringue:	2 tbsp medium ground
8oz/225g/1 cup caster sugar	coffee
4oz/100g/1 cup ground walnuts	6 tbsp sugar
1 tbsp cornflour	4 large egg yolks
4 large egg whites	8oz/250g/2 sticks unsalted butter
Filling:	**Garnish:**
6 tbsp water	9 walnut halves

(serves 8)

To make the meringue: Mix half the sugar with the ground walnuts and cornflour (easiest in a processor after grinding the nuts, but don't reduce to powder, they are nicest with plenty of texture). Whip the whites to stiff peak, then beat in the other half of the sugar by the tablespoonful. Finally, carefully fold in the mixture of sugar, nuts and cornflour. Have three baking trays lined with siliconised, non-stick paper on which you have drawn three 8 in / 20 cm rings. Divide the meringue mixture between these and carefully spread out to fill the circles. Bake in a pre-heated oven at gas mark $1/2$, 250°F, 120°C for $1\frac{1}{2}$ hours, until the meringues are slightly coloured and will lift off the paper. Remove and cool on a wire rack, peeling off the paper. To make the filling: Place the coffee grounds in a small saucepan with the water, bring just up to the boil, remove from the heat, cover and allow to infuse for five minutes. Strain the coffee, return to the cleaned out pan, add the sugar, heat gently until the sugar has melted then boil until the syrup will form a thread when tested between

thumb and finger (236°F, 113°C on a sugar thermometer). Beat the yolks until pale and thick then slowly add the hot syrup, beating all the time, then continue beating until the mixture has cooled.

Cream the butter then gradually add the egg mixture, beating all the time. Spread in between the meringue layers and all over the top and sides of the gâteau. Finish by sprinkling the gâteau with the toasted flaked almonds and chill for 2–3 hours before serving.

Coffee Mille Feuilles

12oz/350g puff pastry	3 fl oz/100ml/¹/₃ cup
Filling:	double cream, chilled
3 egg yolks	1¹/₂oz/40g/3 tbsp icing
2oz/50g/4 tbsp sugar	sugar, sifted
3 tbsp cornflour	Icing:
pinch salt	4oz/100g/1 cup icing
8 fl oz/250ml/1 cup milk	sugar, sifted
2 tbsp coffee, freshly ground	approx. 1 tbsp water
	1oz/25g bitter chocolate

Roll out the puff pastry into a rectangle which, trimmed, will measure 8 x 18 in / 20 x 45 cm and ¹/₁₀ in / 2mm thick. With a sharp, heavy knife cut into three identical strips, 6 x 8 in / 15 x 20 cm. Place upside down on a large greased baking sheet brushed with water. Prick the strips all over with a fork to prevent them rising too much and bake in a pre-heated oven at gas mark 7, 425°F, 220°C for 20 minutes or until puffed and a good, hazelnut brown. Place pastry on a wire rack to cool.

To make the filling, beat egg yolks with sugar until thick and pale then beat in cornflour and salt. Heat the milk with the coffee to boiling point, allow to infuse for 2 minutes then

strain and pour into the beaten yolks and sugar, stirring
constantly. Place in a clean saucepan and, stirring all the time
over a medium heat, bring mixture to the boil. Lower heat
and simmer carefully for 2–3 minutes until mixture thick and
smooth, watch that it doesn't scorch on the bottom. Pour
into a clean bowl and beat with a balloon whisk until cool. Add
the icing sugar to the chilled double cream and whisk in a
chilled bowl until the mixture will almost hold its shape. Add
the pastry cream and carefully fold both together.

To assemble: Place the strips of pastry on top of each other
and trim the edges with a sharp knife. Then place on upside
down on a rack and spread with half of the cream. Turn the
second strip upside down and place on top, spread remaining
cream on top and place last strip upside down on top, making
sure it is quite level.

To ice: Melt chocolate. Stir sufficient water into the icing
sugar to make a thick and smooth icing. Take out two
tablespoons and add to the melted chocolate, stir together
well then place in small paper bag and cut a tiny piece off the
point to make a piping hole. Spread the white icing over the
top puff pastry layer then pipe lines of chocolate icing across
the top, $1/2$ in / 1 cm apart. Run a wet skewer across the lines
in alternate directions, 1 in / 2.5 cm apart. Leave to set, then
serve.

Coffee and Walnut Cake

Many years ago, Fullers in England sold a coffee and walnut cake
with a white frosted icing. The following recipe brings back
memories of that very popular cake.

5oz/125g/generous 1/2 cup butter, softened
8oz/225g/1 cup caster sugar
2 egg yolks
3 tbsp coffee essence
3oz/75g/3/4 cup walnuts, roughly chopped
5 fl oz/120ml/1/2 cup milk
8oz/225g/2 cups flour sifted· with 3 tsp baking powder and a pinch salt
2 egg whites

Frosting:
10oz/275g/1 1/2 cups sugar
4 tbsp water
1/4 tsp cream of tartar
pinch salt
2 egg whites

Garnish:
8 walnut halves

Cream the butter then beat in the sugar until mixture very light and fluffy. Beat in egg yolks and coffee essence then the chopped walnuts. Fold in the flour and milk, together, in three lots. Whip whites to soft peak and fold carefully into the mixture. Pour into two greased 8 in / 20 cm sandwich tins and bake in pre-heated oven at gas mark 5, 375°F, 190°C for 20—30 minutes, until risen and springy. Leave in tin for five minutes then turn out onto wire rack to cool.

Frosting: Mix together the sugar, water, cream of tartar, salt and egg white, stirring until sugar dissolved, then place over a pan of simmering water and beat until the mixture will stand in peaks. Remove bowl from heat and continue beating as the mixture cools until it is stiff enough to spread. Spread just under half on one of the cake halves, top with the other then spread remaining frosting all over cake. Decorate with the walnut halves and leave to set.

Coffee Macaroons

These unusual macaroons are as delectably moist and toothsome as the more common variety.

6oz/150g/^{2}/₃ cup ground almonds
10oz/275g/1^1/₂ cups caster sugar
4 tbsp instant coffee powder (grind coffee granules)
3 egg whites, lightly beaten to break up

1^1/₂ tbsp arrowroot or rice flour
^{1}/₂ tsp vanilla essence
rice paper
split almonds

(makes 16)

Mix together the almonds, sugar and coffee powder. Add the egg whites and beat together well. Stir in the arrowroot or rice flour and the vanilla essence. Place rice paper on baking sheets then spoon on dessertspoons of mixture, spreading out to about 2 in/ 5 cm across. Leave plenty of room between the rounds for further spreading. Add a split almond in the middle of each round. Bake in a pre-heated oven at gas mark 4, 350°F, 180°C for about 20 minutes. Leave to cool on the baking sheet then break off rice paper around each macaroon and store them in an airtight tin.

Coffee Banana Bread

Somewhere between a loaf and a cake, this is a useful and tasty teatime treat that can be served with or without butter.

8oz/225g/2 cups self-raising flour, sifted with pinch of salt

2 tbsp roughly chopped walnuts
4 tbsp very strong black coffee
2 ripe bananas, mashed

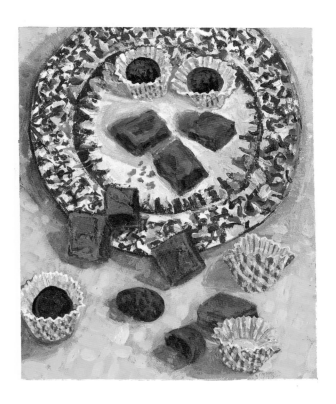

| 4oz/100g/¹/₂ cup butter, diced | 2 large eggs, lightly beaten |
| 6oz/175g/1¹/₄ cups soft brown sugar | 2 tsp ground coffee mixed with 2 tbsp demerara sugar |

Rub the butter into the flour with fingertips until the mixture resembles breadcrumbs, stir in the sugar and the chopped walnuts. In another bowl, mix together the coffee, mashed bananas and eggs then mix this with dry ingredients, stirring until you have a smooth mixture. Line a greased 2 lb / 1 kg (9 x 5 in / 22.5 x 12.5 cm) loaf tin with a strip of non-stick baking paper covering the bottom and ends and pour in the mixture. Sprinkle the mixture of ground coffee and demerara sugar on top and bake in a pre-heated oven at gas mark 4, 350°F, 180°C for 1–1¹/₄ hours or until the cake is springy to the touch and an inserted skewer emerges clean. Allow to cool in the tin then store in an airtight container. The loaf is best the day after baking.

Coffee and Rum Truffles

The finishing touch to a great meal.

7oz/200g bitter chocolate	3¹/₂ fl oz/100ml double cream
2 tbsp rum	2–3 tbsp icing sugar, sifted
4 tsp coffee essence	cocoa powder
(makes approx. 24)	

Melt chocolate with rum and coffee essence in a bowl over a pan of simmering water. Remove from heat, gradually beat in cream and then icing sugar to taste. Cool then beat until mixture is the consistency of thick cream, and will stand in peaks. Refrigerate until stiff enough to shape into balls. Toss teaspoons of mixture in cocoa powder and, between palms of hands, roll in more cocoa. Keep in fridge and consume within one week.

Index